Dreams Do Come Tr[ue]

Tina Hayes
2019

Getting Ahead With Etiquette

Roadmap to Success
for Young Adults, Teens
and College Students

Cheemah
PUBLISHING

Cheemah PUBLISHING
Oakley, California
www.CheemahPublishing.com

Printed in the United States of America

Testimonials

Mrs. Hayes,

During your College Preparedness Training Workshop, my son Garrett learned a tremendous amount of information required to excel in both his college and professional careers. Prior to attending, the word "etiquette" triggered thoughts of the "Good Old Days" and he felt it may not apply to his life today. After completing the workshop, he realized that the practices of proper social conduct apply as much today as it did in days gone by. Thanks so much for polishing his skills!

--Wanda Ransom

Dear Mrs. Hayes,

We are forever grateful for the etiquette training you provided for the Miss Spelman College Contestants. It is imperative as maturing, young women to be aware of how to properly carry ourselves in professional settings. Your skill-set ranging from personal interactions, to dining etiquette and proper decorum in initial conversations, will carry over to many arenas. After being chosen as representatives of Spelman College, we will employ your teachings to an even greater degree. The numerous appearances, speaking engagements, and service opportunities will benefit from our participation in your class. Words cannot express how deeply honored we are to have met and worked with you in such an intimate setting. Your aura and immediate excitement is what captivated each of us. You came into all of our lives leaving a piece of yourself in each of our hearts and we are forever grateful. The two days we spent with you were filled with learning, laughter, joy, and most of all love! Ms. Hayes thank you from the bottom of our hearts for making a difference in each and every one of our lives! Thank you again for providing such essential skills to our personal and professional development.

--Raavin Evans and Deloris Wilson

Thank you so much for your Etiquette training class for my daughter! After completion of the youth "Growing For Success" etiquette class with Ms. Tina Hayes and staff, I see an improved Antonia in that she thinks before reacting while at the dinner table. In restaurants, she exhibits exemplary dining decorum and at home, she enthusiastically insists on setting the dinner table for all holidays and special dining events. Her knowledge and confidence of where silverware, plates, bowls, napkins and drinking goblets are to be set is a work of art! She even folds napkins beautifully! Furthermore, the fact that she is aware of the proper way to display manners in public is a huge success.

--Mrs. Green

I enjoyed everything about the class because I learned something new each class session. There was not anything that I didn't enjoy; it was a good experience. At first I thought that there wasn't much to etiquette, but this class has opened my eyes to how important etiquette is.

--Hilltop Christian School (Teen Student)

Dear Mrs. Tina,

Thank you so much for all of your advice and instructions. I am so fortunate to be privy to some of your knowledge and wisdom. I know that I will use what I learned for years to come. I look forward to further training on etiquette and decorum.

--Chelsea Shaffer

Dear Mrs. Tina,

Thanks for the opportunity to train with you and be a part of the College Preparedness Etiquette training class. I have learned how to present myself to others, meet new people, dorm room etiquette, how to dine in a mannerly way and much more. You are great at what you do. I will leave for college knowing what "soft-skills" are and how to use them. Because of my etiquette training with you, I will be successful.

--Lateefah Edmondson

Table of Contents

Acknowledgements

To my family... a very special thank you to my husband & unofficial editor, **Mark Hayes**; my son and motivator, **Michael**; and my daughter and right-hand, **Cameron**. I love you all very much and appreciate the support given to me and The School of Etiquette and Decorum.

How fortunate I am to have worked with the finest book coach in the world: Cyndee Paulson-Heer. Her relentless faith in my writing has kept me going. She's been a teacher, motivator, and dear friend. Cyndee, because of you, I Did It! Thank you from the bottom of my heart.

DeeDee Buserwini and Mark Heer, I am much appreciative to you for your editorial guidance and proofreading. My gratitude to Douglas Silva of *Midnite Graphics* for his artistic vision and design work for the book jacket. My heartfelt thanks go to these special contributors: Dustin Paulson Heer, Teena Green, Lateefah Edmondson, Chelsea Shaffer, Wanda Ransom, Deloris Wilson, Raavin Evans, and Theresa Price of the National College Resources Foundation.

I could not have taken this journey without the constant support, encouragement and motivation from family, special friends and my mentor. I am so grateful to all of you: mom, Ethel Oakley; sister and operations manager, Tangela Holmes; best friend of 30 years, Tawanda Duck; best friend and business concierge, Veronice Becton; mentor, Mrs. Peggy Newfield, founder and president of The American School of Protocol, Atlanta. I want to also thank my publicist and friend, V. Sheree Williams, who continues to "push" me to higher heights. Each of you has played an important role in helping me live out my dreams. It is challenging at times, but I'm enjoying the journey. "Dreams Do Come True."

Thanks to my Lord and Savior, Jesus Christ for the vision. How blessed I am that He continues to provide all that I require.

And to you... Thank you for reading **Getting Ahead With Etiquette.**

Foreword
By Cyndee Paulson-Heer

I met Tina at a networking event. She was as polished as she was beautiful. Her smile radiated and her eyes sparkled. It was easy to connect with her and I found her to be delightful. Over a period of about one year our paths crossed multiple times. Even though I considered myself as one who knew a lot about etiquette, I decided to take one of her classes. It proved to be both informative and enjoyable.

I initially thought of etiquette as a set of "courtesies" that guide "proper" behavior. I enjoyed it, and always loved the old-fashioned movies that portrayed that set of skills, but I was also left with a feeling that etiquette was for "stuffy" people. To my surprise and enjoyment, working with Tina opened my eyes to a whole new understanding. When Tina contracted me as her book-coach and publisher, I embraced her vision of reaching teens and young adults with this set of skills so that they can improve their confidence, connections, and open more personal and professional doors.

Tina is a boomer girl. She grew up in Richmond, California. She was not born with a silver spoon. She worked her way through college and into a job that stretched her beyond her comfortable limits. Driven by her determination she set out to learn the skills that would help her grow and feel more at ease and confident in her new world. She learned how to dress, how to present herself in various situations, and how to start and maintain a conversation.

By learning these skills Tina was able to improve herself and open new doors.

Throughout her book, Tina breaks through out-dated thinking about etiquette and brings her reader into the 21st century telling why and how it is relevant to the quality of one's life. She spotlights a world without etiquette: i.e. sneezing, coughing, belching, speaking loudly, and using inappropriate language in public. She builds etiquette upon a foundation of consideration, self-respect, and respect for others, and shows how it can enhance your world, and move you closer to your goals.

When you break life down, it is based upon a series of relationships, not only with people, but with concepts, beliefs, thoughts, and things (material objects such as our cars, houses). The meaning we give to these relationships string together to form our beliefs, fears, passions, and values; they, in turn, form our view of the world and shape our attitudes. Our attitudes drive our thoughts and behaviors, close or open doors for each of us, and influence what we do when we walk through a particular door. In bringing you "Getting Ahead with Etiquette", it is our *hope* that you will soften your heart, develop these social-skills, and interact with people and life in a "soft" respectful way. Through this process, you will make better connections and build better relationships because it is from that place of softness that you discover your true-self, and create yourself and your life with purpose and intention.

Introduction

Getting Ahead with Etiquette is my gift to teens and young adults. My main purpose for writing this book is to help you understand how you can get ahead with a set of soft-skills called etiquette. In a competitive marketplace, understanding and exhibiting proper etiquette behaviors will give you a "leg up" in the professional world, and keep you a step ahead of others.

In reading my story, you can better understand how etiquette was the underlying component to my success.

My name is Tina Hayes. This is my story . . .

High School Years - I was raised in Richmond, California. As a teenager, I never considered myself smart; therefore, I dedicated much time to my studies. As a result, I earned high grades and graduated with honors in just three years. What an experience to graduate as a Junior!

College - Following high school, I immediately went to college, California Polytechnic State University, San Luis Obispo, to study Graphic Arts. During my five year college tenure, I changed majors and schools. In 1985, I graduated with a Bachelor of Science degree in Business from California State University, Hayward. I then married my high school sweetheart and we had two children.

Career - After graduation, I was hired as a Personnel Supervisor for a temporary agency. I was responsible for interviewing candidates for temporary work assignments. After two years, I went to work for a small corporation performing a variety of accounting and administrative functions.

My next job was with a large corporation where I worked for 17 years in a variety of positions. The majority of these positions were in accounting; however, I also assisted with College Recruiting and worked as a Training Coordinator. I was hired as an entry level accountant, and then worked my way into accounting management. *Through my "actions" and self presentation skills I earned a good reputation.* Working as an accountant in Corporate America was not easy for me. To compensate for my lack of technical (accounting) skills and knowledge, I developed strong business soft-skills (personal qualities, habits, attitudes and social graces that make a person a good employee and compatible to work with).

I brought to work a positive attitude. I dressed professionally. I took pride in my work. I was reliable and kept a good attendance record. I was courteous, a team player, and considerate of how I treated others. I also showed a high level of respect toward others and easily adapted to new situations and challenges.

One of the requirements of my first management position involved travel and attending meetings where I had to represent the company I worked for in both business and social settings. When I first began attending these meetings, I felt intimidated and under-qualified. I was unfamiliar with business protocol outside of the office and I lacked networking skills.

I was often faced with situations which required me to mingle and connect with people I didn't know. I will never forget how uncomfortable I felt walking into a convention hall with more than 300 strangers and having to start a conversation.

Oh, and the feeling of defeat when I dined at the formal dinners held in huge, beautiful, five star ballrooms. I was awed by the nice china place settings, crystal glassware, chandeliers and cloth napkins but had no idea how to present myself or how to eat in that type of fancy environment: I didn't know which fork to use, how to hold my fork and knife correctly or how to properly cut my food.

Here I was a College Graduate, in management, and making a lot of money; however, I could not "dine" properly! Could you imagine my embarrassment? . . . a*nd that is putting it mildly*!

As a result of these experiences, I eventually developed strong social, business, and dining etiquette skills. The set of skills I developed softened and refined me. I grew more comfortable within myself. I also grew in confidence and success. It is now my goal to teach you these soft-skills so that you will never have to feel uncomfortable and awkward in social and professional environments.

The success that I have achieved is the result of my soft-skills, and how I interact with, and present myself to others. Etiquette is not about the ability to look sophisticated. It is about a set of skills that can refine you, help you better connect with others, be more comfortable with yourself, and feel more confident.

I truly believe that every person reading this book will learn tools to be more successful and accomplish great things in life. That is my wish for you!

Tina Hayes

~1~

The Value and History of Etiquette

Many people think etiquette is a list of rules that tell us how we should behave. These rules are loaded with many expectations that, if not understood, can put some people off. The list includes such things as:

- Chew with your mouth closed.
- Cover your mouth when you cough.
- Keep your elbows off the table.
- Say excuse me when you belch.
- Shake someone's hand when you meet them.

Most people have learned that the above gestures are the Proper and Polite things to do to show respect for others and to behave in a respectful manner; however, it goes much deeper.

Etiquette is about Consideration and Respect.

Proper Etiquette will:

- Change the way people view and treat you.
- Help you gain the respect of others.
- Build self-esteem, self-confidence, and self-respect.
- Help you step into another's shoes, and connect you with how you would like to be treated.
- Teach you how to behave and help you feel at ease in a variety of environments including Social, Dining, Networking, and Professional Situations.
- Help you feel more comfortable around people of varying social backgrounds.

The soft-skills of Etiquette can help you open and grow as a person, and soften you so you can experience more fullness of life. **Etiquette can open doors for you.**

A World without Etiquette

What would the world look like without etiquette?

- Selfish, boorish, uncivilized behavior.
- People sneezing and coughing without covering their mouths, possibly spreading disease.
- People talking loudly on their cell-phones.
- There would be no **"Please," "Thank You"** or **"After You."**

What is Etiquette?

The Webster Dictionary definition of Et-i-quette is *1. the forms, manners, and ceremonies established by convention as acceptable or required in social relations, in a profession, or in official life. 2. the rules for such forms, manners, and ceremonies.*

Etiquette, therefore, is the set of social rules we live by, to show respect toward others and ourselves. In its most simplistic form, etiquette is defined as, "The rules that guide people's behaviors."

Etiquette is Not:

- Some old-fashioned set of rules that is not needed or used anymore.
- Something that is taught only in finishing schools.
- A set of behaviors associated only with dining.

Some History about Etiquette:

Much of today's formal etiquette originated in the French Royal Court during the 1600's. King Louis XIV did not appreciate people walking on his lawn and through his garden during his parties; therefore, he had signs or tickets posted everywhere to guide his guests as to where to walk and how to conduct themselves at his functions. These signs and tickets were the beginning of Etiquette.

Etiquette is a French word meaning Ticket.
One can think of Etiquette as their
Ticket to Success

Etiquette can open doors to a world of possibilities.

Chapter Highlights

_____

_____

_____

_____

_____

_____

_____

_____

_____

_____

_____

_____

_____

_____

_____

_____

_____

_____

_____

_____

_____

_____

~ 2 ~

First Impressions

It is part of the human condition to assess and draw conclusions about people and situations. It is so natural that our first assessments are drawn within seven seconds of meeting someone. This chapter is about First Impressions and Putting Your Best Foot Forward. Chances are you have heard it said that "First impressions are lasting ones, so make them count!" Make it your GOAL to leave a Positive First Impression, and you will build a respectful reputation and a network of quality connections.

First Impressions are formed from your Overall Appearance and Demeanor.

The following list will help you pinpoint areas that you can control in helping make a good first impression:

Clothes:
- Make sure your clothes are clean, pressed, and fit properly.

- Dress appropriately for the occasion.

Hair:
- Make sure your hair is washed and neatly combed.
- Style it appropriately for the occasion.

Approachability:
- Smile. A warm smile has a pleasant effect on others.
- Be friendly and approachable.

Posture:
- Sit and stand respectfully.
- Do not look at the ground. Hold your head up.
- Do not slouch. Stand with Confidence—Proper upright posture conveys confidence. It will not only lengthen your body, but it can also boost your spirits.

Speech:
- Enunciate your words clearly.
- Commit to expand your vocabulary on an ongoing basis.
- Pay attention to the way you articulate, improve where you can.
- Limit the use of slang and use it ONLY when appropriate.

Self Presentation Skills:

- Extend a proper handshake.
- Genuinely smile.
- Make eye contact.
- Control nervous gestures (nervous knee bouncing, pen clicking, playing with your hair, scratching, nail biting or cracking knuckles).

Note: Research shows that body language, including your posture and nonverbal communication, is responsible for 90% of your message. In other words, people pay more attention to how you act, sit and stand than what you say. Focus on that first impression.

Some tips to help you with good body posture:

- Exercise regularly to strengthen your bones and core.
- When appropriate, view yourself in the mirror, taking note of how you stand.
- Pay attention to how you sit in casual situations, and make small adjustments to improve your posture naturally.

"You Never Get a Second Chance to Make a First Impression"

Chapter Highlights

_____

_____

_____

_____

_____

_____

_____

_____

_____

_____

_____

_____

_____

_____

_____

_____

_____

_____

_____

_____

_____

~ 3 ~

Communication Skills & Mingling

Good communication skills are essential for personal and professional success. People who can carry on a conversation, understand, and articulate a point well, will often find themselves amongst the most popular and sought after groups. These skills include the ability to start and carry-on a conversation, non-verbal communication, and style.

- How comfortable are you attending social events? . . . Alone?
- Are you comfortable walking up to someone and starting a conversation?
- Do you have trouble keeping a conversation going?
- When you engage in a conversation, do you often feel like you are saying the wrong things?

If you struggle with the aforementioned questions, you are not alone. You are, in fact, with the majority of the population. There is only a small amount of the community that find it easy and enjoyable to mingle with people they do not know. I consider myself a socialite. I have been on both sides of the fence and sometimes become uneasy when networking or attending social events.

During some period in your life, you will need to mingle or network with others. To help you feel more comfortable, I have included some tips and strategies that will help you navigate social situations with more ease.

How to Start a Conversation:

Start a conversation with **Small Talk**. Talk about the event you are attending, the weather, current events, or give an honest, sincere compliment. Never start a conversation with a Negative Comment!

Below are some suggestions to break the ice and start a conversation.

- "Hello. My name is Tina. I'm a student at Hayes School. I'm really enjoying the event. How is your experience so far?"
- "Hi. This is a nice conference. The workshops are really good. I think they did a fabulous job putting this together. What do you think?"
- "I adore the necklace you're wearing. It compliments your outfit nicely. Let me introduce myself. My name is Tina Hayes."

- "I'm new to the school and I'm looking for ways to meet other people. Are there any organizations or clubs that you can recommend?"

Once Engaged in a Conversation:

- Make direct, but soft eye contact.
- Listen.
- Do not allow your mind to wander. Stay present and connected with the person with whom you are engaged in conversation.
- Do not fold your arms in front of you.
- Ask open ended questions: How did you become involved with our organization? Tell me about . . . ?
- Ask for an opinion. (People love when you ask for their opinion).
- Share comments and follow up with questions. (That's interesting . . . Tell me more).
- Observe how your listener reacts when you're talking. (Are you boring them or do they want to hear more?).
- Have a calm cadence. (Don't talk too slowly and don't speed talk either).
- Don't monopolize a conversation--allow others to contribute.
- Don't ask deep personal questions.
- Avoid discussions on topics that spark emotions such as politics and religion.

How to End a Conversation:

If you need to end a conversation, you can say:
- "This is a very interesting conversation. I would love to hear more. However, it's getting late and I need to leave."
- "Please excuse me? I would like to get a bite to eat."
- "I'm enjoying our conversation. However, I see a friend I would like to talk with."
- "Let me call you so we can continue this at another time."

"Communication - the human connection—
is the key to personal and career success."
Paul J. Meyer

Chapter Highlights

_____

_____

_____

_____

_____

_____

_____

_____

_____

_____

_____

_____

_____

_____

_____

_____

_____

_____

_____

~4~

Public Speaking

Chances are you will not escape the need, at some point in your life, to "take the podium." Whether it is to give a presentation, lead a meeting, or simply make a public toast. The better prepared for it you are, the more comfortable with it you will be.

In my profession, I am often required to speak publicly. Like many others, I experience anxiety. You can be your own coach. You can rally yourself to a confident state of mind. To help manage the worry, I use some of the following techniques:

Positive Self-Talk:

- "I'm confident."
- "I'm prepared."
- "I'm releasing the anxiety."
- "What I have to say will benefit someone in the audience."
- "The more I speak, the better I become."

- "I'm taking steps toward becoming a powerful speaker."
- "I trust myself."

Take Deep Breaths:

- Breathe deeply. When people are nervous, they tend to take very shallow breaths. This deprives you of oxygen and intensifies the fear. Concentrate on relaxed, deep breathing. This will ground you and elevate your confidence.
- 15-20 minutes of cardio, before speaking, will help clear your head and boost your confidence, lower your blood-pressure, and deepen your breathing.

Know your Subject Matter and Your Audience:

- Memorize your opening and closing lines and make them memorable.
- Make sure you know a few things about your audience so you can direct the content of your speech toward them, and connect with them.
- Look for what your audience and you have in common, and speak to that as it pertains to your subject.
- If possible, speak on topics with which you are familiar.
- Prepare and Rehearse, Rehearse, Rehearse--there is nothing better to boost confidence and put you

at ease than preparing and rehearsing what you will talk about.

- Don't worry about being perfect, just do your best.
- Practice in front of a mirror or tape yourself.

Connect with Your Audience:

- Stand tall and confidently with good posture.
- Take several seconds to connect with members of the audience before you begin speaking.
- Engage your audience in your opening statements—you can open with a couple of relevant questions.
- Briefly share something about yourself as it relates to your subject.
- As you speak, make brief eye contact with as many of the audience members as possible, and speak directly to people.
- Smile when you talk.
- Be yourself.

The audience wants you to succeed as much as you do. Come from a serving heart, and you will do well!

Chapter Highlights

_____

_____

_____

_____

_____

_____

_____

_____

_____

_____

_____

_____

_____

_____

_____

_____

_____

_____

~ 5 ~

General Dining Etiquette

Have you ever shared a table with someone who stuffed their mouth so full they looked like a chipmunk? Worse yet, that someone started talking, sending food particles flying in your direction! They may have even used their sleeve as a napkin or talked so loud it sounded like they were yelling.

In a fine dining situation, have you ever wondered:

- Why are there so many forks?
- Which one do I use first?
- Which glass is mine?
- What do I do with the napkin after I finish my meal?
- That's my bread plate... I think?

Long ago, we were taught the answers to these questions, either at the dinner table or in school. Today, schools place more emphasis on sports than manners, and table etiquette is rarely taught in the home. Does this mean that etiquette is no longer important for those of us living in the 21st Century? No! To the contrary, knowing proper dining etiquette is as important today as it was hundreds of years ago. Etiquette plays a significant role in how we are viewed by others, and our dining decorum is a visible display of our manners. Knowing proper table mannerisms is not only important for the teen experiencing his or her first date, the bride and groom on their wedding day, the business professional, or the politician, but also the casual diner.

Here are some tips to help you become table savvy and make a good impression:

- Upon arrival at the table, greet other guests and introduce yourself. Do not shout across the table to a guest. It is impolite! If you wish to address someone further away, at a large table, walk around and position yourself within arm's reach of them.

- In formal settings, remain standing until the host or hostess has been seated—a gentleman should seat his female guest first (she will be seated to the right of him).

- Use good posture while seated at the table: chin above your plate and hands generally in your lap. Elbows are sometimes permitted on the table if no food is in front of you; however, my personal preference is to keep them off the table.

- Do not place personal belongings on the table. Small purses should be placed on one's lap, under the napkin; larger bags on the floor.

- Now, even though you may be famished, do not begin eating until everyone has been served. If you are dining buffet style, wait until at least half of the diners have returned before indulging.

- When passing containers with handles, set it down on the table with the handle facing the recipient.
- The salt and pepper shakers are married. They travel in pairs. If someone asks you to pass the salt, you also pass the pepper.
- Don't blow coffee or soup, just let it set a minute.
- Condiments such as ketchup and mustard should be placed on your plate then use a knife to apply to foods such as hamburgers and sandwiches.
- Bread board with bread – Place a napkin over the bread before you cut it. Don't use your hands. After you cut the bread, pass it to the person on your right before taking some. *Really? You can't take a piece?*
- Once you have used a utensil, do not place it on the table. Don't even put it partly on the table and partly on your plate.
- Cut one bite of meat at a time. Don't pre-cut your entire meal first.

Napkin Etiquette:

The napkin is one of the most important tools at the table. It is used to start the meal, end the meal, wipe your mouth and fingers, and catch crumbs.

To begin a meal, the small luncheon napkin (usually a paper napkin) should be completely unfolded, whereas the large dinner napkin (18-24 inches) should be folded in half and placed in your lap. Never place your napkin in your shirt to be used as a bib. The napkin remains in your lap throughout the meal. If you have to leave the table during the meal, place the napkin on the back of the chair or on the table (try to conceal the soiled side). Do not put it on the seat of the chair. If the napkin falls to the floor, do not pick it up, just ask the waiter for another one. Once you have completed your meal, neatly place the napkin to the left of your plate.

Dining etiquette applies to all dining experiences, whether you are eating at home, a guest at someone's home, Ruth's Chris Steak House or your local McDonald's.

How you do anything is how you do everything –
be the example your friends would like to emulate.

Chapter Highlights

_____

_____

_____

_____

_____

_____

_____

_____

_____

_____

_____

_____

_____

_____

_____

_____

_____

_____

_____

_____

~ 6 ~

Table Setting and Navigation

My mentor once told me that a proper and beautifully set table makes the meal taste better. That may or may not be true, but it certainly adds to the ambiance and can increase one's appreciation for the dining experience as a whole.

The following list will help you with formal table setting and navigation.

- The **Dinner Plate** is always positioned in the center of the place setting, preferably on top of a decorative service plate/charger, place mat, or nicely pressed table cloth.
- The smaller **Salad Plate** goes on top of the dinner plate and used only when the salad is served as a separate course.
- The **Dinner Fork** & **Salad Fork** are located to the left of the plate. In formal settings, the salad is traditionally served before the main course;

therefore, the salad fork is positioned to the left of the dinner fork.

- The **Dinner Knife, Salad Knife** and **Soup Spoon** are placed on the right side of the plate. The soup spoon is placed farthest right, then the salad knife, followed by the dinner knife, which is nearest to the plate (the blades of the knives face the plate). *The rule for silverware is to use the utensils from the outside in as the meal progresses.*
- The **Dessert Spoon** and **Dessert Fork** are laid horizontally above the plate, the fork below with the handle to the left, the spoon above with the handle to the right.

Please note – only set the table with utensils that will be needed during the meal. For example, if no soup will be served, do not set your table with a soup spoon.

- The **Napkin** is neatly arranged to the left of the plate or on the plate: <u>Never under utensils</u>. A creative option is to fold the napkins into a stylish shape.
- If bread or dinner rolls will be served, the **Bread Plate** is placed just above the forks. The **Butter Knife** is positioned horizontally across the bread plate (blade facing diner).
- The **Glassware** is located to the right of the plate above the knives. Five is the maximum amount of glasses one can have at an individual place setting:

water glass, white & red wine glasses, champagne glass & sherry glass.

- **Coffee Cups and Saucers** are not to be placed at a formal setting. After the main meal is completed and the dishes removed, the coffee cups are brought in, in preparation of dessert service.

Here are some easy tips to help you remember that the bread plate and forks go on the left, and the glasses, spoon & knives on the right.

b d (Bread & Drink):

Hold both hands in front of you, palms facing each other. Using the tips of your thumb and forefinger, make circles on each hand. The remaining three fingers in each hand point upwards. Your left hand forms a "b" and your right hand forms a "d". Bread(b) is on the left, and Drink(d) is on the right.

Fork, Spoon & Knife:

FORK has four letters, so does LEFT; SPOON & KNIFE have five letters, so does RIGHT.
Fork left, spoon and knife right.

BMW:

Bread(B) left, Meal(M) center, and Water(W) right**.**

The basic principles of table setting will also help you when you are dining out. Practice setting the table, so when you're attending banquets, weddings, and other extravagant events, you will feel comfortable knowing which fork to use first and which glass and bread plate is yours.

Bon Appétit! That is French for "Enjoy your Meal!"

Chapter Highlights

_____

_____

_____

_____

_____

_____

_____

_____

_____

_____

_____

_____

_____

_____

_____

_____

_____

_____

_____

_____

_____

~7~

Soup Etiquette

"Just like ships go out to sea, I spoon my soup away from me." This is one of those sayings that grandmothers used to teach their children the correct way to eat soup.

Can you believe it? There is even a proper way to eat soup.

Just for fun, pause and think about the way you currently eat a bowl of soup. Chances are you drop your head toward the bowl, spoon the soup inward toward your body, blow, slurp, eat. I'll bet you even leave the spoon in the bowl when you are finished.

If the aforementioned practice seems normal, I invite you to review the following tips on soup etiquette.

Soup Etiquette:

- Don't bend your head toward the soup bowl; rather, slightly bend inward from the base of your spine without slumping. Keep your back straight and raise the spoon all the way up to your mouth.

- When eating soup, spoon away from your body. Enter bowl from the front and move to the back of the bowl, allowing the spoon to wipe the back rim of the dish. There are a few exceptions, one being French onion soup which is spooned inward.

- Soups are not to be blown. If the soup is hot, patiently wait 1-2 minutes, and then fill the spoon, skimming from the top of the soup.

- Clear soups, broths, and heartier soups are eaten by placing the spoon, point first, in the mouth. No slurping allowed.

- Crackers are not to be crumbled into soups; however, oyster crackers can be enjoyed in chowders.

- Soups should be served with the soup bowl on a plate underneath. When you finish your soup, leave the spoon on the plate, not in the soup bowl or on the table cloth.

- Soups served in a cup with two handles (lug soup bowl) can be picked up and drunk (after you use your spoon to eat the chanterelle on top).

Next time you indulge in a warm, hearty bowl of soup, practice proper soup decorum. You just might enjoy the polished feeling that accompanies such etiquette.

Chapter Highlights

_____

_____

_____

_____

_____

_____

_____

_____

_____

_____

_____

_____

_____

_____

_____

_____

_____

_____

_____

~ 8 ~

Home Dining

"Mark! Michael! Cameron! Dinner is ready!" How often do households hear the echoing sound of their mother's voice calling them to the dinner table today?

Family dining is becoming a lost art. What a shame. We are not only losing an opportunity to connect and share the highlights of our day, but the dinner table was once a place where manners and dining etiquette were taught. In days gone by, a mother could be seen demonstrating to her children the proper way to cut food, and a dad, most often, could be heard scolding his son for not washing his hands before arriving at the table.

Here are some tips to help you better connect at the dinner table and sharpen your dining etiquette:

- Wash your hands before arriving at the table.
- When called to eat, arrive <u>immediately</u>. Do not make others wait or make special arrangements to keep the food warm.

- Turn off the television. Really tune in to each other and connect. Enjoy conversing with one another. This is a great time to learn about how each person spent their day.
- Start and end meals together. No one should leave the table until all are finished.
- Keep dinner time sacred. Do not talk about dieting, or anything of an argumentative nature. These issues can be handled at another time. Make dinner time a time to connect and engage in pleasant conversation.
- Say "please", and "thank-you" when requesting or receiving foods or dining amenities.
- Don't make negative comments about the food. Out of respect try at least one bite of each dish (past experiences or looks can sometimes be deceiving).
- Take medium to small bites when eating and chew foods well.
- Never talk with food in your mouth.
- Never place dirty utensils on the table. When a utensil is not in use, place it completely on your plate.
- Don't use toothpicks at the table. Excuse yourself to the restroom if something gets lodged in your teeth.
- <u>Always</u> pay a special compliment to the cook after the meal (even if it's a family member that cooks daily). Compliments reassure people and express

appreciation to them. Compliments also pay dividends down the road!

- Remove your plate from the table and offer to help with the dishes.

For those Sunday Dinners spent with extended family and close friends, here are some additional key points to remember.

- Invited guest should arrive at the appointed time. Never too early or no more than 10 minutes late.
- Invited guest should bring the host or host family a small gift of appreciation.
- If eating buffet style, wait until at least half of the diners are seated at the table before you start eating.
- When passing foods, pass to the right (counter-clockwise). Also place the dish on the table versus placing it in another's hands (this helps avoid spills and burns).
- If something spills, don't make a big fuss about it. Clean it up and continue the meal. If you are the person who caused the incident, apologize and offer to help clean it up.
- In a casual dining environment, it is okay to eat fried chicken with your fingers; however in a formal setting, use a fork and knife.

Just a thought...

Make dining together an experience everyone looks forward to. Connect with each other and spend time practicing and polishing your dining etiquette.

Chapter Highlights

_____

_____

_____

_____

_____

_____

_____

_____

_____

_____

_____

_____

_____

_____

_____

_____

_____

_____

_____

~ 9 ~

Dining Out

Once while visiting my son in college, I had the pleasure of dining out with my etiquette teacher, mentor and friend, Mrs. Peggy Newfield, President and Founder of The American School of Protocol® in Atlanta. We arranged to meet at a restaurant in Buckhead (a region of Atlanta). Feeling slightly apprehensive and wanting to make an exemplary impression, we (my son, a soon to be college graduate, and I) arrived early. After reserving a table, I experienced a lapse in memory and was unsure as to whether we should be seated at our table or wait for Mrs. Newfield in the lobby. I decided upon the latter.

The restaurant began filling up and upon hearing the host state that the Friday "rush" would be starting soon, I decided to be escorted to our table. Once seated, I knew to leave the napkin on the table and not drink, eat or order until my special guest arrived. Our server came and introduced herself. I mentioned that we were expecting another guest and informed her that I would be handling the bill. Peggy soon arrived. We stood and handled the proper protocol through introductions and greetings. We enjoyed a fabulous lunch and first-class decorum was exhibited throughout the meal.

This experience prompted me to share some tips on restaurant etiquette and social dining.

Restaurant Dining Protocol:

- Make reservation well in advance. If you are unable to honor a reservation, place a cancellation courtesy call.
- Introductions and greetings should be made while standing.
- If you find that your dining utensils are dirty, ask the server to replace them. Do not clean tableware in a restaurant.
- Protocol states that you should order the same number of courses as the majority of the guests at the table. If others are ordering appetizers, salads, soups or desserts, follow suit.
- When excusing yourself from the table, do so after you have placed your order or between courses.
- Wait until all are served before you begin eating your meal.
- When dining buffet style, wait until at least half of the guests have returned to the table before you indulge.
- Iced Tea – stir quietly using a half moon motion. Your neighbors at the surrounding tables should not hear you stirring your beverage.

- Avoid loud conversations and be respectful of other diners.
- Tasting other's entrées is acceptable as long as it is done at the beginning of the meal, before any silverware is used. Pass your bread plate to the person whose food you want to taste and let them cut a small bite and place it on your bread plate.
- Ice is never to be chewed in public.
- Toothpicks and dental floss are not to be used in public places. If something is lodged in between your teeth, excuse yourself to the restroom and handle it there.
- When you finish your meal, don't push your plate away to indicate that you're finished. Just wait for the waiter to come and remove it.
- The standard tip is 15%-18%. In upscale restaurants, 20% is customary. If you will be spending an extended amount of time at your table, leave more than the standard tip. Take into consideration the additional customers your waiter could have served.
- Never call attention to the dining mistakes of others or be overly apologetic about your own.
- Do remember to thank the hostess, waiter, or chef.

Home Affairs with Friends:

- R.S.V.P. in a timely manner to allow the host to prepare properly. Also when responding, you can obtain additional information about the event. i.e.— dress attire, what to bring, etc.

- Bring the host a small gift; however show discretion when presenting and don't bring items that require a lot of immediate attention. i.e.—flowers requiring a vase.
- Be timely and don't overstay your visit. Adhere to the times on the invitation.
- Refrain from bringing uninvited guests.
- Inform the host if you accidently break or spill something.
- After the event, make sure you express your gratitude by sending a timely note of appreciation.

How to Handle the Bill When Dining Out with Friends:

You are dining out with friends and having a great time. The meal is delicious, the conversation interesting and the atmosphere lively. Later, the bill arrives along with the awkwardness of how to split it. Someone has to take charge and oversee the payment. It's too late to ask for separate checks. Now what? Do you split the bill equally, ask everyone to pay an approximate amount for what they ordered, or pull out the phone calculator and have everyone pay the exact amount?

To simplify this matter, agree on how you will handle it before anyone orders.

Below are the three most common options for handling the bill.

Splitting the Bill Evenly:

When using this option, the bill is split evenly amongst all diners (Two couples - Total cost $50, each couple renders $25). The advantages are that bill division is quick and easy to calculate. This method is preferred when people do not want to hassle over the cost or when several dishes, appetizers and beverages (bottled wine) are shared. There are two main disadvantages: the bill is usually higher, and people tend to use less caution when making selections, often ordering more expensive items. The result is that everyone ends up paying more. If you are on a budget and watching your expenses, this is not a favorable solution.

Separate Checks:

This is the most fair, efficient, and accurate method. Diners pay only for what they order. No one feels cheated, taken advantage of or under obligation to bear other's expenses.

Why is this method not used exclusively?
1. Some restaurants, mainly upscale establishments, do not allow tables to have separate checks.
2. Shared items such as bottled wines and appetizers cannot easily be separated on individual bills. *Also consider the scenario when you order a starter and everyone else indulges. Will you be okay or will you feel "slighted."*

3. This is not a favorable option for congratulatory meals, such as birthdays, when the guest of honor's meal is compensated by the entire group. The honored guest should not be made to feel uncomfortable when much discussion is centered on the division of their tab.

Pay Only for What You Ordered:

Paying "only" for what you ordered is a common method used to divide the bill in casual dining situations. The diners pay an approximate (usually rounded up for convenience) amount for their meal and beverage, including tip and tax (25%-28%). When using this method, someone must "step up to the plate," oversee the process, and handle the details. The primary advantage to using this approach is that the disparity between the actual amounts and what is paid is minimal.

If you find yourself in a situation where no one is making a move for the bill, quietly pick it up and review your portion. Fairly calculate, round up, and pay your total. Then pass the bill to another stating, "This should cover my share."

Over the course of your lifetime, chances are that you will use all forms of bill division. The method you choose will depend upon the variables of the individual dining experience. I cannot say that any method is best or that fairness will always play out when dividing the bill. There is no way to escape those occasions where you will pay more than your share, but knowing your options will limit those occasions, and make dividing the restaurant bill easier.

"Breaking bread" together is a common way to connect in our society. Knowing your options for dividing the bill will keep you out of the monetary concern, and in the dining experience.

Chapter Highlights

_____

_____

_____

_____

_____

_____

_____

_____

_____

_____

_____

_____

_____

_____

_____

_____

_____

_____

_____

_____

~ 10 ~

Etiquette in Public Places

Have you ever been annoyed by the mannerisms or lack of decorum by people in public places? Have you ever thought or even made the comment "someone needs to teach him/her some manners?"

When attending a public event: a concert, the theater, a sporting event, or museum, your manners are on display. Being courteous and respectful toward others is essential. Many etiquette experts share the opinion that the Golden Rule—"*Treating others the way you would like to be treated*" is the single best guide to follow when interacting with people.

When in doubt, however, here are some simple guidelines to help you reflect respectable behaviors in public places:

- Make an effort to be considerate of others.
- Hold the door open for the person behind you.
- Do not have your friend save a space in line for 10 other people.

- Arrive on time for events to avoid bumping and crawling over people. (If you must pass over those seated, say "excuse me" or "I'm sorry" and pass facing the person. It's better to see one's face then their back side).

Theater & Concert Etiquette:

- Keep your feet on the floor. Do not put them on the seats around you.
- When talking, keep your voice low or wait until intermissions or between performances.
- Don't draw attention to yourself by shouting loud comments or booing performers.
- At concerts refrain from singing along or humming unless asked to by the performer. You may have been blessed with a beautiful voice, but others paid to hear the headliner.
- Follow the established rules of the venue.
- If food and drink are not allowed, don't sneak them in.
- If food and drink are allowed, clean up your area before leaving, and properly discard trash.
- Where there is assigned seating, always sit in the proper seat.
- If you end up with an extra ticket because your friend "bailed" at the last minute, consider making someone's day and offering the ticket free of charge. It will cast you in a good light and make

you feel good about yourself. Also, keep in mind that scalping tickets is against the law, and you could end up being detained and miss the performance.

Sidewalks, Doors & Elevators:

- When walking on the sidewalk with friends, if a passerby approaches, move to the side, and do not make it difficult for the person to pass.
- As you walk through doors, always check behind you; if the opportunity exists, graciously hold the door open for others.
- Allow people to exit an elevator before you enter. If you are situated near the control panels, offer to punch in the floor buttons for those entering.

Clubbing:

- ALWAYS play it safe when drinking. ALWAYS assign someone in your party to be a "designated driver."
- Watch your alcohol consumption level so that you do not make a spectacle of yourself. (Enjoy yourself, responsibly). Some clubs require a two drink minimal. Your beverage does not have to include alcohol. A *virgin daiquiri is my favorite.*

Be aware of your surroundings and consider the feelings of others; shared experiences should be pleasurable for all.

Chapter Highlights

_____

_____

_____

_____

_____

_____

_____

_____

_____

_____

_____

_____

_____

_____

_____

_____

_____

_____

~ 11 ~

Cellular Phone Etiquette

Cellular phones are everyone's "best friend." We "don't leave home without them." While they can help keep us connected, they can also cause "a disconnect" with the people we are with, and, if not used politely, can cause a disturbance for those around us.

Basic Cellular Phone Etiquette:

- Trust voicemail features. Unless a call is urgent, allow callers to be directed to your voicemail.
- When attending to business or personal affairs on your phone, speak soft enough so as to not disturb those around you.
- If you have a bad connection, either excuse yourself to a place where you can elevate your voice or call the person back at a better time. (I have heard one sided conversations concerning intimate relationships, family issues, and even pet concerns). "Forcing" others to listen to your affairs is highly disrespectful.

- To retrieve messages and return calls, in public, find a private or otherwise appropriate environment.
- Even though the selections and availability of ringtones are limitless, use discretion when choosing one. (Ringtones, just like the clothing you wear, are a reflection of your taste and character). Think about the message you are sending?
- Set the ringer to an acceptable volume, just loud enough for you to hear from your purse or pocket. Better yet, use the vibrate function.

Voicemail Etiquette:

- Your outgoing message should be brief, friendly, and easy to understand.
- Tell your callers exactly what you want them to do to leave a message and how it will be handled. For example, you can leave a message like this: "Hello, you have reached Tina Hayes. I'm not available. Leave a message along with your telephone number, and I will return the call as soon as possible." Smile as you record your message. It will come across in your voice and reflect a friendly demeanor.

Please note: It is in poor taste to require callers to listen to long inserts of your favorite songs before being allowed to leave a message.

Event Cellular Phone Etiquette:

- Honor the rules as laid out by the venue or host at public events.
- When requested to turn off your phone, respond immediately!
- Turn your phone off when entering places such as a theater, church, airplane, doctor's office, beauty/barber shop, library or classroom, and even your gym.

It is inappropriate to use a cellular phone while dining in restaurants and even at fast-food establishments. It cannot only be annoying to your dining companions; it can be disruptive to nearby diners that might be celebrating a special occasion. If you are awaiting an important call, inform your dining companions ahead of time, set your phone on vibrate, then excuse yourself from the table when the call comes through.

The majority of Americans own and use a cellular phone. The advancement of technology has allowed us to communicate freely with almost no limitations. It is important to adhere to proper etiquette and show courtesy when using your phone in public. These rules were not developed to place more limitations on you, but to make public places more respectful and equally enjoyable for all.

Take extra precautions to keep your conversations private. Be considerate of those in close vicinities. Never yell while using your phone in public, and make sure your emotions are under control. Finally, be mindful of small children and refrain from the use of profanity.

Make a conscious effort to observe etiquette as it relates to using your cell phone in public and we can all stay more pleasantly connected.

Chapter Highlights

_____

_____

_____

_____

_____

_____

_____

_____

_____

_____

_____

_____

_____

_____

_____

_____

_____

_____

_____

_____

~12~

Travel Etiquette

The best or the worst can be seen in people while traveling. Begin your journey with an amiable attitude and pack your manners. Travel with a high level of decorum and you'll be surprised by the superior level of service you'll receive. People will welcome you everywhere.

To help ensure the best in your travels, refer to the guidelines and etiquette listed below:

Air Travel:

- Be Timely – Arrive at the airport in plenty of time to avoid the frustration and stress of rushing.
- Be Patient – Expect long lines and endure them without complaining.
- Exercise Self Control.
    - Don't blame the airline personnel if the flight is delayed
    - Politely follow directions in the security lines.

- o When boarding and deplaning, proceed as instructed. Hurrying to obtain your carry-ons and lingering in the aisles will not help you off the plane any faster.
- o Alert the flight attendants if you have a tight connection as special arrangements can be made.
- o Show consideration for people sitting near you. Respect their space.
- o Share the armrest (the middle seat should be granted access).
- o Position your chair so that both you and your neighbors are comfortable.
- o Be cognizant of the noise you may make.
- o When listening to iPods and talking with travel companions, keep the volume low.
- o If you occupy an aisle seat, be understanding when others need to pass.
- o Don't bring smelly foods or wear strong fragrances on the flight.
- o Smile and show some appreciation for airline staff.

Whether traveling with family, friends or alone,
the attitude you take with you will make
or break your experience.

ACCOMMODATIONS

Before you Travel:

- When your travel involves an overnight stay in a hotel, familiarize yourself with the accommodations and amenities of the hotel and surrounding area.
    - Does the guestroom have a hair dryer, iron, coffee service, etc.?
    - Does the guestroom have a television, cable, internet?
        - Is there an additional fee for internet?
    - Are there fees for telephone calls and movie rentals?
    - Does the guestroom have a refrigerator and/or microwave?
    - Does the hotel have a business center?
    - Is there a gym or access to a nearby fitness center?
    - Does the hotel have "in house" laundry services, restaurant/s, gift shop/s or anything else you might need? (Some hotels are elaborate enough to include a movie theatre, bowling alley, and a variety of spa facilities).
    - Are there restaurants within walking distance?

Upon Arrival:

- Once checked in, survey your room for towels, blankets, pillows, hangers, etc. If you need additional items, call immediately to avoid delays. It's better to request housekeeping during the day than wait until late at night when the services are limited.
- Follow the rules of the establishment. For example, when staying in a non-smoking room, avoid smoking.
- Keep noise to a minimum. Be aware of the television and radio volumes; most rooms are in close proximity of one another and separated by a very thin wall.

Note: It is okay to take the unused portions of the shampoos, conditioners, lotions, etc. The towels, robes, mugs and glasses, however, are for your enjoyment only during your stay. Taking them is considered stealing.

Tipping Guidelines:

- Bellman: $1-2 per bag.
- Valet Parking: $2 when your car is retrieved.
- Doorman: $2 for hailing a cab.
- Maid Service: $2-5 per night. (Place tips in a marked envelope labeled housekeeping and then leave on a pillow, desk area, or in the bathroom).

- Room Service: the gratuity is usually added to the bill, if not, tip 18%-20%.

When tipping, have the exact change ready. Do not put yourself in a position to ask for change. This is considered tacky!

Traveling Abroad:

There is much to be said about international travel. It can be fun, educational, and for the unseasoned world traveler, a bit daunting. Before you pack your bags, familiarize yourself with the local customs and practices— they can differ from area to area. If you do not know the language of the locals, at the very minimum, learn the following words or phrases: "Please," "Thank-you," "Hello," "I don't understand," "How do you get to?" For those of you who love to shop, add the question: "How much does it cost?"

Learning these word and phrases will take you far when traveling to foreign countries. You can also expand the experience and your connection with locals by using an English Translation Dictionary. This shows them that you care about and respect their culture.

English	Chinese – (Cantonese & Mandarin)	French	German	Japanese	Spanish
Hello	Ne ho Ni hao	Bonjour	Hallo	Konnichi wa	Hola
Please	Cheng Qing	Sil vous plait	Bitte	Kudasai	Por favor
Thank-You	M goi Xie Xie	Merci	Danke schon	Arigato	Gracias
Excuse Me	Chengmahn Qingwen	Pardonnez-moi	Entschuldigen-Sie	Sumimasen	Dispense me

Pack your best smile. It can be your passport to an astounding travel experience and lead you on an adventure beyond your wildest imagination.

Chapter Highlights

_____

_____

_____

_____

_____

_____

_____

_____

_____

_____

_____

_____

_____

_____

_____

_____

_____

~ 13 ~

Choosing a College

Why should you attend a College Fair?

Never will you find a better opportunity to "shop colleges" than at a College Fair. As many as 150 colleges can gather in one place for YOUR convenience. Sure they want to sell you on their school, but if you have done your homework and know what YOU want, you can narrow the prospects and briefly interview the recruiter to see what they offer to YOU.

What is the Objective of the College Recruiters?

- To share information about the college.
- To generate interest in their schools.
- To recruit students (Remember these recruiters are also salespeople, so do your homework).

Below is a questionnaire, created by the National College Resources Foundation for their annual Black College Expo™. It has been included to help you interview recruiters.

- How can I arrange a campus visit? Are there any special visitations days on your campus?
- What are the application deadlines for admissions and financial aid?
  - What scholarship programs am I eligible for at your school? (Presidential, Community, Leadership, etc.)
  - How do you assign faculty advisors to students, especially those who are undecided about their major?
  - When must I choose a major?
  - What percentage of students commute? (If the school is a commuter school).
  - What types of extra-curricular activities are available on campus?
  - How accessible are the professors outside of class?
  - What is the student to professor ratio?
  - How are roommates selected?
  - What additional academic services do you offer to students? (Tutoring, career counseling, and study skills workshops).
  - What types of internship/ co-op experiences are available?

- How safe is your school? (Parking lot lighting, emergency call centers, night shuttles).
- Where can I obtain statistics about crimes on your campus?
- What are the annual tuition rates?
- What is your school known for? (School's specialty).

Let me add two more:
- What is your National Ranking?

My personal favorite:
- What do I need to know to be the best student your school has ever educated?

Choosing the right school is important for your personal and academic success. Take time to connect with the BIG Vision of your life, and what YOU want. Then you will be ready to interview college recruiters and get the most out of your efforts.

In the end it is about you, your education,
your career path . . . your character, your legacy.

Chapter Highlights

_____

_____

_____

_____

_____

_____

_____

_____

_____

_____

_____

_____

_____

_____

_____

_____

_____

_____

_____

~*14*~

The College Experience

College is a new and exciting time in your life. It is the period when you transition from Adolescence to Adulthood. It is a time when you start to define yourself beyond your peers and family influences. It's your chance to consider who you truly aspire to be, and take action toward becoming that person.

Helpful Tips for College Success:

School:
- Attend your College Orientation & become familiar with your school's website.
- Develop relationships with administration & staff.
- Your advisor should know you by name.
- Introduce yourself to ALL of your professors during your first few day of class—a simple *"I am honored to be in your class, and I'm looking forward to what you'll be teaching me"* will do.
- Sit in the front of the class—*the first 2 rows*.
- Study hard and don't hesitate to ask for help.

- Make friends who are focused on success.
  - Meet with them regularly.
- Get involved with a campus activity, club, or organization.
- Study Abroad.

Finances:

- Learn to manage your finances.
  - Don't waste extra money eating at restaurants.
  - Make a budget for each semester and stick to it.
  - Buy used books or purchase books from upperclassmen.
  - Make your meal money count as described above.
  - Don't forget to allocate money for entertainment.

Personal Development:

- Keep a journal.
  - Get curious about who you are and what you want to accomplish in life.
  - Make a list of ALL the things you want to do, personally and professionally.
  - Reflect on who you are, who you want to become, and the legacy you want to leave.
  - Make a list of ALL the characteristics with which you want to be identified.

- o Take time to create a personal vision for your life, and chart how you might get there—be flexible with the "how" of it.
- o Track your challenges and look for ways to overcome them.
- o Track your Successes and celebrate them.
- o Capture the highlights of your days and your experiences, focusing on your favorite parts, and what you love about them.
- o Be flexible with the experiences of life and stay open to the "learning's" each has to offer.

Socializing:

- Don't become distraught if people don't always agree with you or if they act totally different. You can learn from these differences and expand your own horizons.
- Don't conform to other people's ways just to fit in. Be yourself!
- Use caution when socializing.
  - o Don't drink with people you don't know.
  - o Don't party too much.
- Follow the "Golden Rule."
  - o Treat your roommate and others with the utmost respect.

Balance:

- Balance your time and resources.
  - o Eat balanced meals and take <u>full</u> advantage of the cafeteria and your meal plan.

- o Maintain a fitness program that includes cardio.
- o Don't over study.
- o Get an adequate amount of sleep and relaxation.
- o Schedule clean, fun entertainment.
- Try new things.
  - o Push beyond your comfort zone and you just might discover "the next best you."
- Be flexible and enjoy the journey.

College can be a joyful time. Learning can be fun.
Keep your eye on your ultimate goals.
Balance your behavior and enjoy the journey.

Chapter Highlights

_____

_____

_____

_____

_____

_____

_____

_____

_____

_____

_____

_____

_____

_____

_____

_____

_____

_____

_____

～ 15 ～

Dorm Room Etiquette

For many college students, especially freshmen, dormitory living brings about some distress. You leave the comfortable surroundings of your home and family and have to share a small space with a complete stranger. We all grow up with different values, habits and philosophies and there is bound to be some culture shock. Getting along with your roommate is essential and the best way to create a peaceful atmosphere is through mutual RESPECT and CONSIDERATION.

Listed below are some simple guidelines to help you create a peaceful relationship and enjoy your dorm room experience:

- Keep your area clean. It is unlikely that your school will offer maid service; therefore, it is your responsibility to clean up after yourself. Don't throw your clothes around. Make a special effort to make your bed daily. Take out your food trash to avoid smelly odors, ants, roaches, and rodents.

- Show respect when your roommate is sleeping or studying. This is not the time to invite friends over, blast music, or engage in a lengthy phone conversation.

- Get to know and respect your roommate's schedule. If you wake-up earlier or keep later hours, make an effort to keep the noise level low.

- Never borrow your roommate's belongings without asking. Make sure you monitor your guests and do not allow them to handle your roommate's stuff. *Your guests are your responsibility.*

- Keep valuable items locked away. Lock your room when you leave, even if it is just to go down the hall. *You don't want anyone stealing your roommate's items during your watch.*

- Communicate! If you are having "issues," discuss it with each other. Don't gossip and don't spread rumors about your roommate.

- Consider writing a **roommate contract.** The agreement can allow each of you to openly discuss likes, dislikes, habits, and preferences early on before conflict arises. Establishing rules on how each of you would like to be treated helps eliminate problems.

Sharing a living space and learning to get along with others is part of the college experience. How successful will you be? By adhering to aforementioned tips and treating your roommate with the highest degree of respect and consideration, you can enjoy dorm living!

It takes effort and determination to live in harmony with others.

Chapter Highlights

_____

_____

_____

_____

_____

_____

_____

_____

_____

_____

_____

_____

_____

_____

_____

_____

_____

_____

_____

~ *16* ~

Classroom Etiquette

Many students/parents spending thousands of dollars for their own/their child's education want to get the most out of their investment. While learning can occur anywhere and everywhere, the classroom is an important part of the educational experience, and should, therefore, be respected as such. But learning is primarily the student's responsibility. Attitude will take you far. Not only should you, the student, bring a desire to learn, but you should also be eager and take full responsibility for your education.

Following are some guidelines and tips to help you adapt within the classroom, and optimize the learning process:

- **Present yourself suitably to your instructors**. Introduce yourself, and provide some background information on yourself, so your professors may become better acquainted with you. Extend a proper handshake and express gratitude for the opportunity to be in their class.

- **Arrive at the classroom on time.** If arriving late, do not be a distraction to the class. Sit in the first vacant seat nearest the entrance.

- **Come prepared for class.** Bring assignments and class materials such as textbooks, pens, paper, etc. Review the class syllabus before you arrive and ALWAYS do your homework.

- **Contact your professor ahead of time if you have to miss a class.** Be sure to make arrangements to obtain the lecture notes and assignments.

- **Pay attention when the instructor is teaching.** Participate in class discussions, however, do not dominate the discussion or constantly interrupt the teacher to make a point.

- **Know when to approach your teacher.** The best times are before and after class or preferably during office hours to obtain extra help.

- **Silence your cellular phone.** If you cannot turn it off during class, keep it on silence and ignore it during class time. Do not answer your phone, send or receive text messages.

- **The classroom is for learning not eating.** Although some professors may tolerate coffee or lite snacks in the classroom, be cognizant of the distraction that they may cause for other students. Smelly and crunchy foods, for example, should be prohibited. Also, be careful not to spill your drink.

- **Do not wear heavy perfumes or colognes to class.** Some students are sensitive to them, and may even have an allergic reaction.

Just a thought . . .

What is the PURPOSE of Attending School if not TO LEARN?

Chapter Highlights

_____

_____

_____

_____

_____

_____

_____

_____

_____

_____

_____

_____

_____

_____

_____

_____

_____

_____

_____

_____

~ 17 ~

Dating Etiquette

Dating can be a rewarding experience. The "restaurant" date, being one of the most common, provides intimacy in a social setting and affords two people the opportunity to get to know one another, but it can also bring-up discomfort around "proper behavior." Proper conduct on dates is natural for some and awkward for others. When you are familiar with the basic rules of conduct it makes it easier to trust your behavior, relax, enjoy yourself, and keep your attention on the romance.

Below is a list of tips that will not only help first-time daters feel more confident and at ease, but will help generate a renewed connection for seasoned couples.

- **Plan ahead**: When making reservations, choose a location that can help set the "tone" for your date. If it's a first date, select a setting where you can talk and get to know each other.

- **Dress appropriate for the occasion:** Remember first impressions count. If in doubt, call the venue in advance for the dress code and don't be afraid to splash on a little extra cologne *or perfume.* *I love it when my husband dresses up and splashes on a little extra cologne. It adds some spice and excitement to the evening.*

- **Be on time**: Impress your date by being punctual. (Ladies, if he's picking you up, be ready. Gentlemen, arrive promptly at the appointed time).

- **Compliment one another:** If someone compliments you, accept it with a smile and say "thank you." (Many people can offer nice accolades but have problems receiving them. Refrain from explaining why you don't deserve the compliment).

- **Keep the conversation lively**: Talk, laugh, and reminisce. Make sure you make direct but gentle eye contact.

Note: Some people struggle to start a conversation. Below is a short list of questions and inquiries to help you initiate a chat or restart it if you find yourself in one of those moments of awkward silence.

- o What do you do in your free time?
- o Tell me a little bit about your family.
- o Is there anything you've always wanted to do, but haven't had the chance?
- o Tell me about your favorite movie.

- **Use proper table manners:** (for a refresher on dining, see chapters 5 - 9).

- **Keep pace with your date:** Do not eat too fast or too slow.
- **Be sensitive to the payee's pocketbook**: During menu selection, the ladies can inquire about what their date will be ordering to gauge pricing. During the first couple of dates, I advise against ordering the most expensive items on the menu.
- **Always bring money/credit card on a date**: No matter what arrangements have been made, don't go empty handed. Have a back-up plan.
- **Allow chivalrous conduct:** This means that the ladies will allow the men to be gentlemen. Chivalrous behaviors includes the male:
  - Pulling the chair out for his date and gently pushing it back in after she is seated.
  - Walking behind the lady when lead to the table by the maitre d'.
  - Paying for the meal.
  - Placing the order for the lady once she makes her meal selection by saying, "the lady will have..."
  - Opening and closing building and car doors for the lady.

Some of you may think these suggestions are old-fashioned and out-dated; however, a little extra attention goes a long way to make someone feel special.

- **Thank your date** at the conclusion of the evening regardless of the quality of the experience. Words of gratitude are polite and always welcomed.

Going out on a date can be expensive, even an outing as simple as dinner and a movie.
Enjoy the experience and the time that you have with each other. Make each moment worthwhile.

Chapter Highlights

_____

_____

_____

_____

_____

_____

_____

_____

_____

_____

_____

_____

_____

_____

_____

_____

_____

_____

~ 18 ~

Wedding Proposal Etiquette

The story of the wedding proposal is one of those stories that we love to share. It is deeply special to most couples and reflects a distinctive moment. If you conduct a survey, you will find that most couples remember their marriage proposal down to the smallest detail.

The "storybook" proposal involves a balance between romance and creativity. To help make yours memorable, I have included some suggestions and guidelines.

- Adhere to tradition by informing her parents of your intentions. This shows respect. (Hopefully, you have established a positive relationship and will receive their blessings).
- Most couples have had some discussion on the subject, but a proposal should still be somewhat of a surprise. This helps make it memorable.
- Even though the groom does all the planning

surrounding the proposal, he should be sensitive to the taste and personality of the bride-to-be, and make it something that will make her happy. (*Will she prefer an elaborate or simplistic approach?*)

- The proposal should include a ring. If you are unsure of her ring size and taste, make sure your purchase is with a reputable jeweler that allows exchanges.

- Regardless of the flair, or lack thereof, surrounding the proposal, there needs to be some degree of formality: Drop to one knee. Tell her why you want to marry her and then ask, "Will You Marry Me?"

- Do not make her uncomfortable by putting her on the spot and demanding an immediate response.

- Don't be offended if she asks for time to consider your proposal. Some women prefer to contemplate such important decisions. Keep in mind that you had time to reflect on the subject before proposing. Give her the same consideration.

- Keep your proposal intimate and private. How embarrassing it would be to have your proposal rejected in front of others.

The wedding proposal is one of the most precious moments in a couple's life. Spend time to make yours delightful and memorable.

Chapter Highlights

_____

_____

_____

_____

_____

_____

_____

_____

_____

_____

_____

_____

_____

_____

_____

_____

_____

_____

_____

~ 19 ~

Wedding Etiquette

The Wedding Experience regardless of size is a *magical* moment in a couple's life. Planning it is time consuming and tedious and can take months. Many couples choose to contract a Wedding Planner. To help you better understand some of the basic logistics before, during, and after the "Big Day," I have included a list of things to consider before you invest in that stack of wedding "How-to Books."

Bride & Groom:

- Surround yourself with people who will support your decisions about your wedding day.
- Strongly consider using a wedding coordinator (even if they're just to oversee the ceremony).
- Peggy Newfield, founder and owner of The American School of Protocol in Atlanta, and my mentor and friend, offers the following suggestion. Make sure all the clothes for your special day, especially undergarments and shoes, are worn

before the ceremony so you know that they are comfortable. Nothing is worse than blisters on your feet before the ceremony is over.

- Appropriate gifts to suggest include: flatware, kitchen utensils, crystal, stemware, vases, fine china, candle sticks, frames for wedding pictures, monogrammed towels, bedding, and cookware-- **Do not request money on the invitation**.
- It is okay to return duplicate gifts.
- Show your gratitude in a timely manner. Thank you notes should be written and mailed within three-months and no later than one-year if your wedding was extremely large.
- Grooms, help with the planning process.
- Work as a team. Remember, things happen and not everything and everyone is perfect. Enjoy the experience of planning your wedding, and stay flexible.
- Keep things in perspective. The most important part of your wedding is the ceremony and the joining of two people who are deeply in love.

Bridal Party:

A common misconception amongst the Bridal Party is thinking that their main responsibility centers around walking down the aisle, but their responsibilities go beyond that. The Bridal Party is also the main support team for the bride and groom.

Their responsibilities include:
- Assisting with the planning of the wedding.
- Helping with the arrangements. (Volunteer, don't wait to be asked).
- Be available for all pre-wedding engagements.
- Host showers and/or bachelor parties.
- Be on time. (Don't cause the bride or groom extra stress as a result of tardiness).
- Be the last people to leave the reception.
- Be available to offer words of encouragement during the couple's stressful moments.

The Toast – The person that pays for the wedding gives the first toast (usually the father of the bride). It is also common, however to follow his toast with one from either the Best Man or Maid of Honor.

Things to consider when writing your toast:
- Be sure it's respectful and appropriate.
- Be brief (under a minute or two).
- Prepare for the toast, don't read it from a paper.
- Be sure to include Congratulatory remarks and Best Wishes.

Support and Cooperation are the best gifts that you can give the Bride and Groom. Go along with their decisions. After all ... it is their BIG day!

Guests:

Guest etiquette and responsibilities:
- Consider it an honor to be invited.
- R.S.V.P. – Do not show up if you have not responded to the invitation in a timely manner.
- Only invited guests should attend. Uninvited guests are considered "Wedding Crashers." It is very inappropriate to "crash" a wedding.
- As an invited guest, you are obligated to give a gift. Traditionally, all gifts are to be sent to the bride's home before the day of the wedding. Within some regions and cultures, it is acceptable to bring the gift to the reception. The grace period for giving a gift is one year, however it is best to send your gift within three months.
- At the ceremony, the groom's family and friends are seated on the right and the bride's on the left. *Don't forget to be on time.*
- If the social hour is held outside of the banquet room, finish your drink and hors d'oeuvres before entering into the dining hall. It is inappropriate to bring cocktails or sodas to a formal table setting.
- The receiving line affords the bride and groom an opportunity to personally greet their guests. As you proceed down the line, shake hands, introduce yourself, exchange smiles and congratulatory sentiments, and then move along. This is not the time for extended conversations.

- Never re-arrange place cards at the reception; it is a breach of etiquette.

As with any event, the key element to wedding etiquette is to display the highest degree of respect for yourself and others.

Chapter Highlights

_____

_____

_____

_____

_____

_____

_____

_____

_____

_____

_____

_____

_____

_____

_____

_____

_____

_____

_____

_____

_____

~ 20 ~

Thank You Notes

With the internet and texting thank you notes are becoming passé. This is sad because they hold a special place in appreciation and etiquette, and most people love to receive them. Thank you note etiquette involves the acknowledgement of others' generosity. The tangible process of showing gratitude through thank you cards and notes completes the circle of giving and receiving. Failure to acknowledge gifts and good deeds can lead to bad feelings and hurt your relationships. A handwritten thank you note is one of the kindest ways to express your appreciation.

For those of you that dread writing (especially young men), a proper "thank you" is not required to be long and elaborate. It's the thought that counts. Your note can contain as few as 4 sentences.

Below are some guidelines:
- Be specific and personable.
- Acknowledge or appreciation of the gift or deed.

- Share how the gift or deed made you feel or share how the gift will be used.
- Make sure you acknowledge the gift by name. However, for monetary gifts, do not make mention of the specific amount of money. Instead, use wording similar to "I appreciate the generous monetary gift."
- Mention something other than gratitude for the gift.
- Conclude your note with a final remark of greeting and affection.
- Use your best penmanship and mail your card within a week of receiving the gift or deed.

Following is an example of a note written in appreciation for a dinner hosted by a friend:

Dear Cheryl,

I was so surprised and delighted to receive your dinner invitation. It has been a while since we've seen each other. You outdid yourself on the meal. I enjoyed every dish; my favorite was the crab cakes with Cajon sauce. Your culinary schooling is really paying off. So many of our friends and I are anxiously awaiting your graduation and the opening of your restaurant. My fondest appreciation to you for a wonderful evening with great food and friends.

Gratefully yours,

Below is a list of times and experiences that should be acknowledged with a handwritten thank you note; however, it does not have to be limited to these occasions. Use your imagination and expand the list to include other exchanges that you feel are special.

- Graduation Gifts
- Overnight stay at someone's home
- Someone sends you a care package
- Birthday Gifts
- Wedding Gifts
- Job Referrals
- Letters of Recommendation
- Flowers, condolences or donations to the funeral of a family member
- Special acts of kindness

Thank you notes let someone know that their time, effort or good deed was truly appreciated.

Chapter Highlights

_____

_____

_____

_____

_____

_____

_____

_____

_____

_____

_____

_____

_____

_____

_____

_____

_____

_____

~ 21 ~

Being a Guest at Someone's Home

Teenagers and college students are often invited to friend's homes for the weekend and/or holidays. This IS a privilege! In accepting the honor, you are also agreeing to a set of courtesies and responsibilities. It is your duty to be the perfect guest and show a high level of consideration. When you leave, your host should have no concerns about inviting you back.

Courtesies and Responsibilities:

- Do not "make yourself at home!" Even if your host tells you to relax and make yourself at home, DO NOT exercise those freedoms. They are *earned* liberties, and they take time to truly acquire. Instead, bring your best manners and be respectful of your host's home. Do not roam the house freely, open drawers, eat at your leisure, etc.

- Be neat, and clean up after yourself. Do not leave your clothing or personal items scattered around the house.
- Make your bed daily.
- After showering and dressing, ensure that the bathroom is clean and that all your personal items are put away.
- Do not expect the host or hostess to entertain you at all times. If they are busy, find something to do without portraying boredom (i.e.: take a walk or read a book or magazine).
- Always offer to help around the house. If a nice dinner is prepared in your honor, ask if you can help clear the dishes.
- Adhere to the schedules of those you are visiting, as best as you can. Arise and retire (go to bed) around the same time as your host.
- WRITE A THANK YOU NOTE ASAP! It is absolutely mandatory to extend your gratitude for someone allowing you to stay in their home. Do so within one week of your stay.

When visiting someone's home, remember you are a GUEST with responsibilities.

Chapter Highlights

_____

_____

_____

_____

_____

_____

_____

_____

_____

_____

_____

_____

_____

_____

_____

_____

_____

_____

~ 22 ~

Conquering the Hiring Process

It might come as a surprise to learn that there is an art to the interview process, and most of it is about your soft-skills and how you present yourself. According to statistics, your soft-skills and how you are perceived play a major role in your success during an interview. The following section will help you prepare for Interviewing Success, and Conquering the Hiring Process.

Building Your Resume

A resume is your personal ambassador, representing you to a potential employer. It is a tool used to sell oneself on paper. It should be short and descriptive, no more than two pages. It is your first meeting with a potential employer and, therefore, your first impression. According to Wil Lemire, director of career services at Western New England College in Springfield, Massachusetts, "Recruiters typically devote only 10-15 seconds to read any resume. Make yours count and capture their attention."

What to include in your basic resume:

- Personal summary.
- Work experience and education.
- Skills and qualifications.
- Career or job objective, if it's specific.
- Personal strengths and accomplishments.
- Hobbies, skills, and clubs.

What NOT to include on your resume:

- Do not use the word Resume as the subject, at the top of the first page.
- Do not include personal information, such as date of birth, marital status, height, weight, health status, ethnic group or religion.
- Do not include past salaries.
- Do not include past supervisors or other references. You can instead end your resume with the statement "References available upon request." This can also be eliminated if room does not allow for it.

The Professional Summary:

The most important part of your resume is your "Professional Summary." It is equivalent to an elevator pitch. Position the summary just below your contact information. Make sure it is well-written. Unless you lack hard skills, do not waste space listing common skills such as "Good with Word, or Excel." Highlight the things that make you stand out from the crowd.

Things to include:
- Professional and Technical Skills (Hard Skills).
- Personal Attributes, Qualities and Characteristics— think about things that make you easy to be around and work with.
- Degrees, Certificates, Awards and Achievements— only list accomplishments that are relevant to the job in which you are applying.
- Years of Experience.
- Keywords—keywords are words, usually nouns, that are associated with a certain industry, set of skills, certification, etc.
- Additional Accomplishments relevant to the job in which you are applying and that can help "sell yourself" as an asset.

If you lack "Hard Skills" spotlight your Personal Attributes, including things such as:
- Special Talents & Skills.
- Strong Interpersonal Skills.
- Interacts Well with Others.
- Quick Learner.
- Excellent Team Player.
- Computer Training.

- Proficient in Excel, Word and PowerPoint.
- Highlight your Accomplishments:
  - Honor Student.
  - Clubs or Organizations where you served as an executive member.
  - Awards Received.
  - Volunteer Work / Community Service.
  - Internships.
  - Work on Campus.
  - Projects or Research relating to the position you are seeking.

Resume Tips:

- Be Truthful: Never lie on your resume.
- Make it look impressive. It is a reflection of you.
  - Invest in quality paper.
  - Have several people proofread it. A resume must be error free and "perfect."

Note: There are plenty of websites and books that can take you deeper into writing winning resumes. I recommend that you spend some additional time researching a handful before you write yours.

Application:

Some employers require that you fill out an application when applying for a job. This can be in addition to or in lieu of a resume. It's simple and straightforward. When filling out an application, you should be prepared to provide the following information:

- Name, Address, Phone number & Email address.
- Social Security Number.
- Work Experience & Pay rates:
  - Name of Company.
  - Supervisor.
  - Dates worked.
  - Job description.
  - Pay rate.
  - Why you left your previous job/s.
- Your Educational Background.
- Informational questions relating to the position in regards to your interest and qualifications:
  - Why do you want to work for this company?
  - List some of your skills and qualifications that relate to the position.
- Hobbies & Special Interests.
- References.

Before the Interview

Research the company in which you are seeking employment. Find out how long they have been in business, and what their vision, mission and objectives are. This will help confirm if their values are in alignment with yours. It will also help you "speak their language," and finally, it will impress the interviewer.

Phone Message & Social Networking Medias:

Get your house in order. Set your home phone and cell phone up with professional incoming messages just in case a prospective employer calls and reaches your voicemail. You do not want them to hear an embarrassing, childish, slanderous or obnoxious message.

Also make sure your social media presence is professional and clear of any compromising references as some companies examine social networking medias to get a candid sense of a potential hire during the assessment process.

Preparing for the Interview

The more prepared you are for an interview, the more relaxed and confident you will be. The following list is a set of commonly asked questions at interviews. Look them over and consider your answers before the interview.

Typical Interview Questions:

- Tell me about yourself?
- Tell me your strengths and weaknesses?
- Describe your character?
- Why do you want to work here?
- What particular skills and qualities will you bring to the company/position?
- Is there a particular achievement you are proud of?

- What do you know about our company?
- What do you think it takes to be successful in our company?
- Why should I hire you? What sets you apart from everyone else?
- What are your goals for the next 5 years?

Chances are you have heard the saying practice makes perfect. Well, it's no different for the job interview. Practice until you feel comfortable and fluid with your responses.

- Practice!
- Rehearse!
- Participate in a mock interview with a friend— Don't wing it!!
- Make sure you can explain everything on your resume/application.
- Be prepared to give examples of how you would perform the duties of the position in which you are applying.

Sample Questions to ask potential employers—Have at least 4 questions prepared and make sure you understand exactly what you are asking in case the interviewer needs clarification for one of your questions. For example, if you ask them question three below, they may ask "What do you mean?" Make sure you can clarify.

- Can you describe a typical day working at your company based on the position I applied for?

- Can you tell me about the people I will be working with?
- What is your management style?
- Is there potential for me to advance in the company?
- What would be an incentive for me to work here?
- Do you have any concerns or apprehensions that I can clear up that would cause you not to consider me for the position?
- How soon might I expect to hear from you?

Finally, ask for a business card to ensure the correct spelling of the interviewer's name so you can send a thank you note.

Dress for Success:

- Proper, professional attire can consist of the following:
    - Suit or Nice pants & Blouse - Black, navy blue, brown, or gray (basic dark colors are best suited for interviewing). *No hot pink dresses or jeans with a sports jacket.* A light colored shirt preferably white or beige.
    - Neck Tie & Belt to match shoes, for men.
    - Nice Shoes - A dark leather shoe for males and a basic black pump for females. *Make sure your shoes are polished.*
    - Stockings - No designer patterns.

- o Socks – Same color or darker than your pants.
- o Conservative Accessories - Ladies, no dangling earrings.
- o Men are advised not to wear earrings to an interview.
- o Lightly applied make-up, for women.

Additional Dress Tips:

- Make sure your clothing fits well, is cleaned and pressed.
- Don't wear too much cologne or perfume.
- Go the extra mile to ensure that your nails are neatly trimmed and manicured.
- Neatly combed hair.

And don't forget, a pleasant demeanor, your best posture and of course, your confidence.

On Your Way to the Interview:

- Encourage yourself with positive words such as "I can do this," "I'm smart, talented, and highly educated."
- Do some calming deep breathing exercises.
- Envision yourself at the interview doing well.
- Calmly, confidently, rehearse your interview content.

During the Interview

An interview is not just for the company to learn about you, but also for you to learn about the company. Ask questions to ensure the position you are applying for and the company is a good fit for you.

Self Presentation Skills and Selling Yourself in Person:

When you walk into the interviewer's office extend a hand for the all-important handshake.

- Extend your hand and shake, using a firm, not crushing grip.

Wait for the interviewer to offer you a seat. Chances are he or she will proceed to review your resume or application.

- Sit straight and comfortably in your chair, and wait for them to finish their review—do not engage in any nervous gestures.

The interviewer will commence to ask you a variety of questions.

- Smile and maintain comfortable eye-contact.
- Answer questions as succinctly and briefly as possible.

There may be periods of silence whereby the interviewer takes notes and records your responses.

- Wait patiently—do not fidget.

Reference List:

Upon completion of the interview, assuming it went well, the interviewer may ask that you provide references so they can obtain additional information about you.

- Be prepared to furnish at least three references.
- Always ask prior permission from the person you want to use as a reference.
- Keep your references informed of your job-search. This allows them to properly prepare to discuss your accomplishments if contacted.
- Never ask references to lie for you.

You made it through the interview successfully! Now it is time to send a thank you note.

Thank You Note:

Write a thank you note and mail it, preferably within 24-hours of completing the interview.

- There are numerous websites to help you compose your letter:
  - www.thank-you-notes-samples.com
  - www.jobsearch.about.com

Approach the hiring process like a school project: Research, Prepare & Practice.

Chapter Highlights

_____

_____

_____

_____

_____

_____

_____

_____

_____

_____

_____

_____

_____

_____

_____

_____

_____

_____

_____

~ 23 ~

Behaviors & Manners in the Workplace

Harvard University, Stanford Research Institute, and The Carnegie Foundation have all conducted studies which have led to the same conclusion: Getting a job, keeping a job, and getting promoted is based 85% on a person's soft-skills and 15% on ones technical knowledge.

Job etiquette consists of two primary sets of skills: Behavior/Manners and a Good Work Ethic. Behaviors and Manners equate to your interpersonal or soft-skills, your attitude, social graces, and people and job compatibility. Your Work Ethic is about your reliability, integrity and the way you do your Job.

Behavior and Manners:

- Be courteous of shared work spaces, including break-rooms and restrooms.

- Be mindful of your demeanor: be friendly and approachable.
- Dress appropriately for your job. Your appearance is important at work because you represent the company you are working for. The workplace is not the place to "express yourself." You are being paid to express the company you work for.
- Treat co-workers with respect.
- Be mindful of your communications: tone, body language, and word choice.
- Do not gossip about co-workers or complain about management. If you have an issue with something or someone, take it up directly and appropriately with the necessary people.

A Good Work Ethic:

- Be Honest & Hardworking.
- Take Pride in your Work.
  - Strive to be the best at whatever job you do. When you do things to the best of your ability, you feel good about yourself. To achieve this, consistently ask yourself this question, "How would I work if I was the owner?"
- Be Reliable.
  - A reliable person maintains good attendance, is timely, and shows up ready to work. They put in a full day's work and

take all breaks within the scheduled timeframes.

- Work with Integrity.
  - o Be sincere and honest.
- Have a Positive Attitude.
  - o Be enthusiastic and smile often.
  - o Be easy to get along with.
  - o Be willing to help others.
  - o Be productive.
  - o Look for the good in something versus always seeing the bad.
- Be a Good Team Player.
  - o Work hard.
  - o Get along with others.
  - o Focus on the common good and the common goal.
  - o Offer to help others, and don't hesitate to ask for help yourself.

In Conclusion remember:
- Be a model employee.
- Your track record speaks volumes about you.
- Do your best on every job.
- Be a team player.
- Always show respect for others.
- Be customer focused.
- Take pride in your work.

Start each day with a good attitude.
Take it to work with you, whether you are
working part time, full time or on campus.
You never know when you'll need a good reference.

Chapter Highlights

_____

_____

_____

_____

_____

_____

_____

_____

_____

_____

_____

_____

_____

_____

_____

_____

_____

_____

_____

_____

_____

_____

Note Pages

Note Pages

_____

_____

_____

_____

_____

_____

_____

_____

_____

_____

_____

_____

_____

_____

_____

_____

_____

_____

_____

_____

_____

_____

Contact Information

Tina Hayes
The School of Etiquette and Decorum
P.O. Box 4361
Antioch, CA 94531
925-519-0354
THayes@etiquetteschool.us
Etiquette4decorum@yahoo.com
www.etiquetteschool.us

Cover Design by:
Douglas Silva
Midnite Graphics
925-783-0175

Made in the USA
Columbia, SC
27 October 2018